A SPIRIT DAUGHTER WORKBOOK

WRITTEN BY
JILL WINTERSTEEN

———————————

FOR THE FULL MOON

FRIDAY, JULY 23RD, 2021
7:36PM PT

———————————

WHY THE FULL MOON?

Full Moons are powerful and magical times. They reveal our longstanding patterns and show us where we need to energetically shift to manifest our visions. Each Sun Season generally brings us one Full Moon in its opposing sign. This year, we have the rare occurrence of two Full Moons in the sign of Aquarius during Leo Season. The last time we had two Full Moons in the same sign was 2019, which brought us two Libra Full Moons during Aries Season. The lunar cycle does not match the solar year, so every two years or so, the Full Moon lands in the same sign twice. Having two Full Moons in the same sign gives us an opportunity to work with that astrological energy more deeply, along with the energy of the Sun Season.

WHY THE FULL MOON?

There are twelve signs, which are divided into six oppositional pairs. In the sky and on the zodiac wheel, Aries opposes Libra, Taurus opposes Scorpio, Gemini opposes Sagittarius, Cancer opposes Capricorn, Leo opposes Aquarius, and Virgo opposes Pisces. A Sun Season is defined by the sign the Sun is positioned in. For instance, when the Sun lands in Leo, we call it Leo Season. A Full Moon occurs when the Moon lands in the opposing sign of the Sun. This opposition is what allows the Sun's light to be fully reflected from the Moon's surface. The Earth lands in the middle of Sun and Moon, and we get to witness a gorgeous Full Moon. Conversely, the New Moon occurs when the Sun and Moon are in the same sign. During this phase, there is no light on the Moon, making it appear invisible.

Astrological signs are composed of 30 degrees. On the first Full Moon in Aquarius, the Sun will sit in Leo at 1°, while the Moon will sit in Aquarius at 1°. On the second Full Moon in Aquarius, on August 22, the Sun will sit in Leo at 29° and the Moon will sit in Aquarius at 29°. Full Moons that occur at the beginning of a season tend to feel energetically light. They take on energy that is similar to that of a New Moon, marking a transition and giving us a sense of renewal. Full Moons that occur at the end of a season tend to feel more intense, as they occur before the Sun transitions signs. These Full Moons can bring up areas where we feel stuck or confined in some way.

Whenever it occurs in the Sun Season, a Full Moon always gives us an opportunity to do shadow work and begin to learn what lies beneath the surface of our conscious minds. We also have a chance to work with both astrological energies involved. Every energy has a low, or shadow, side and a high side. Zodiac energies bring us both high and low vibrations that correspond to the qualities they govern. We align with these vibrations in different ways throughout our lives. On a Full Moon, we can clearly see and feel how we are embodying the lower frequencies of each sign involved. Once these energies are revealed, we can release and shift them. Each Full Moon brings us the opportunity to transform some piece of ourselves if we are willing to look at our shadows.

As we shift away from lower vibrations, we make room to integrate higher ones. Each opposing zodiac pair has a similar high side. On a Full Moon, we can begin to understand the commonalties of the sign pairs and embrace their higher, integrated vibrations. By doing this, we can raise our own vibrations and clear blocks that prevent us from manifesting our potential.

The first Full Moon in Aquarius begins at the start of Leo Season, when Leo's vibrations are just beginning to affect us. They feel new, and maybe even exciting. Leo Season tends to bring hopeful vibrations as we leave the emotional waters of Cancer. The first Aquarius Full Moon also brings these hopeful energies. It has the potential to show us where we need to transform to embrace the higher vibrations of both of these signs and carry them forward through Leo Season.

The second Full Moon in Aquarius occurs at the end of Leo Season and belongs to the Leo Lunar Cycle, which begins August 8 with the New Moon in Leo. By this point, we will understand Leo's energies well, giving us more to work with this Full Moon. It may even feel more energetically charged as the cosmos gives us a double dose of revelations around Aquarius and Leo.

Enjoy both Aquarius Full Moons fully. Each brings something unique and rare. This event signifies a deep need for the collective to do work in energies governed by Aquarius. Nothing happens by accident in the cosmos. There's a reason everyone on this planet is experiencing this double dose of Aquarius this year. Take the opportunity to reach for the highest vibrations available to you and flow with the extra magic this Leo Season brings us.

AQUARIUS FULL MOON

EMIT THE FREQUENCY YOU WANT TO RECEIVE

Aquarius is one of the more complicated signs of the zodiac, and perhaps one of the most misunderstood. Aquarius at its heart represents the collective. This broad definition includes all the people in a given society, as well as their rules, guidelines, and structures. Aquarius guides our societal norms, along with our definitions of collective terminology, like success, power, and freedom. It also influences group dynamics, including how we treat one another, who leads the collective, and, even more importantly, who changes the rules that govern all of us.

Aquarius governs the collective consciousness, which in its simplest definition is the shared thoughts of a society. You can think of it as a massive cloud that all of society's beliefs, opinions, and energy go into. The collective consciousness influences everyone's thoughts and conditioned patterns, even if they don't realize it. It creates thought paradigms and ingrained belief structures. Some of the collective consciousness can be seen and heard. It appears in advertising, statements from the government, and our social media feeds. While some of the collective consciousness

AQUARIUS FULL MOON

is energetic, it is simply an awareness of what the collective is doing, thinking, and even feeling at any even time. It's a vibration, and we all can tune into its frequency. The collective consciousness is the interconnected web of energy we all live in, and this energy is best understood through the lens of Aquarius.

While Aquarius governs everything having to do with society, it also governs rebellious behavior and individuality. Here is where Aquarius grows more complex. On one hand, Aquarius's energy helps us gather together to form societal structures and training. On the other hand, it also helps us break the structure of society through rebellious acts that challenge the status quo. To reconcile these seemingly opposing energies of Aquarius, we need to understand it as a continuous cycle of evolution. We are hardwired to evolve as human beings. Transformation is one of the primary motivating factors for all behaviors. It is how we went from hunters and gathers to an advanced technological society. Humans want to evolve, and so do the societies they live in. Without change, and without people who demand change, society stagnates.

The energy of Aquarius helps us form a collective group, then it helps individuals find themselves in that group. The ones who evolve past the collective first go on to challenge it. The rebels and the rule-breakers are the ones who ultimately change society. The people who take a chance to be who they are regardless of being accepted by the collective shape the way others live. They are the risk-takers and the people who can see a better future. So, while Aquarius helps us form a society, it also helps us break it down and rebuild. This energy brings out our visions of who we are, who we are within a collective, and what change needs to happen so everyone in the collective feels society is serving them. Aquarius reminds us that we are all connected and that we all breathe the same air. We are all part of the same energetic web, and we are all influenced by the collective consciousness. We also all have a responsibility to contribute to humanity and help evolve it forward through finding out who we are and speaking our truth.

During the Aquarius Full Moon, become keenly aware of how you are influenced by society. How have you been programmed by the world around you? Our societal training comes in many forms. We learn from our parents, our schools, and our peers. Many of our lessons are deliberate, having been thought out by the people teaching them, but many of them are unconscious. In our early stages of development, we are like sponges. We absorb the environment around us and pick up habits, behaviors, and conditioned responses without our awareness or the awareness of the people whose behaviors we are absorbing. We also form concepts by merely living in a world full of other people whose combined knowledge creates the collective consciousness.

Allow this Full Moon to help you find your individual freedom among the collective. What do you need to shed to find your truth? What beliefs are not yours but were merely taught to you? What feels like you and how do you want to share that person with the world? Know that it's ok to change and evolve. Also know that not everyone will be comfortable with your new self. What matters most is that you feel at home in your energy. As you find your truth, speak it. Help change and transform society where it needs to grow. Do this with your words and actions, but also do this with your energy. Notice the energy you are emitting and ask if it reflects who you are. Also ask how it is contributing to the collective consciousness. Feel into your truth this Full Moon, then send it back into the airwaves that shape our shared reality.

(To be continued in the second Aquarius Full Moon workbook.)

AQUARIUS MOON X LEO SUN

As we dive into understanding how to align with Aquarius's vibrations this Full Moon, we also have the opportunity to work more deeply with Leo's energy, where the Sun is positioned. It is the dance between these two astrological frequencies that makes these Full Moons impactful, potent, and transformative. Throughout both Aquarius Full Moons, we are understanding the Leo/Aquarius axis and how to embody it in our own lives.

Leo and Aquarius are two sides of the same coin, and that coin is unconditional love. They may appear opposite in the sky, but these energies are similar in their cores. Their execution of this energy differs, though. Leo governs love on an individual level. This sign guides us in being generous, open-hearted, compassionate, and accepting of love from others while giving it in return. Leo reminds us that the heart is the center of our being and our energy. To live and lead from the heart, we need to express it freely. This authentic expression comes from knowing who we are and accepting every part of ourselves. When we embody the highest expression of Leo, we live a life from the heart; we express our truth freely; and we lead others with compassion, courage, and conviction.

Aquarius, on the other hand, governs love on a more global level. Aquarius reminds us that all beings are deserving of love and each person is worthy of acceptance for who they are among the greater collective. Aquarius inspires us to create systems and structures that serve all people and uphold a love for everyone. From this perspective we can honor each individual's personal freedom while maintaining the structures that hold society together. Aquarius helps us speak our truth when we see inequalities, express our beliefs about how society needs to evolve, and lead our communities forward when needed. When we embody the highest expression of Aquarius, we celebrate the differences among all people while seeing them as equal and worthy of the same unconditional love. Aquarius in its high side gives us a love for humanity while helping us honor each person's individuality.

Throughout both Aquarius Full Moons, we have the opportunity to embrace and integrate the highest manifestations of Leo's and Aquarius's energies. Each sign reminds us that love is the highest vibration of all. And they each help us feel a true sense of belonging with others. Belonging occurs when we can be ourselves around others and feel honored for who we are. Belonging does not require us to mold or bend ourselves to conform to other people's expectations in an effort to find acceptance. True belonging is a product of living authentically and finding others who accept us. When we align with Leo's high side, we gain the courage to be ourselves in all situations and share our hearts' truest expressions. When we integrate this with Aquarius's high sides, we extend acceptance to others as they reveal their true selves. When we feel a true sense of belonging, we can take risks and embrace vulnerability when sharing our ideas with others. We know we are accepted even if others do not completely agree with our ideas; they still value our uniqueness and what we bring to the table. And love is at the center of it all.

During these Full Moons, align with Leo to feel your most authentic self and align with Aquarius to show up in the world as that self, knowing you will find people who appreciate your unique character. Work with these energies to break free of any societal programming that demands that you fit into the status quo. Instead, give yourself the freedom to stand in your truth and share it. This last year has brought us a great opportunity to shift and transform. Now is the time to show those transformations to others. Let other people see how you have changed, even if you're afraid they might not like the new you. Know that some people may not accept you in your truth, and that's ok. What's important is that you remain confident in yourself and aligned with your heart. When you bravely show up in the world with the energy of confidence and integrity, people listen, society listens, and you end up changing the world. It's important, though, to always return to the vibration of love. It will help in your darkest times and return you to the center of your being: the heart. Even when you don't know what to do, the heart will tell you.

The key to embodying the higher vibrations of Leo and Aquarius is releasing their lower frequencies from your field. Every energy has a high side and a low side. These lower, or shadow, sides show up in various parts of life. Through bringing our awareness to these patterns in our behavior, emotions, and energy, we can shift them. We can transform our energy into a higher frequency, unblocking the path to the highest vibration of all: love.

We'll go into great depth about the lower vibrations of Leo and Aquarius in the second Aquarius Full Moon workbook. For this first Aquarius Full Moon, focus on feeling who you are and sharing that person with the world. Feel into what blocks you from being yourself and practice full acceptance of others when they reveal their true selves. Does the same thing that prevents you from accepting yourself prevent you from accepting others? How does it feel to show your true self to the collective? Where are you holding back your truth, and how can you free your voice? Release old patterns and training that tell you that you have to be a certain way to be accepted. Challenge these outdated narratives and be who you are right now, in full acceptance of yourself and others.

HOUSESCOPES

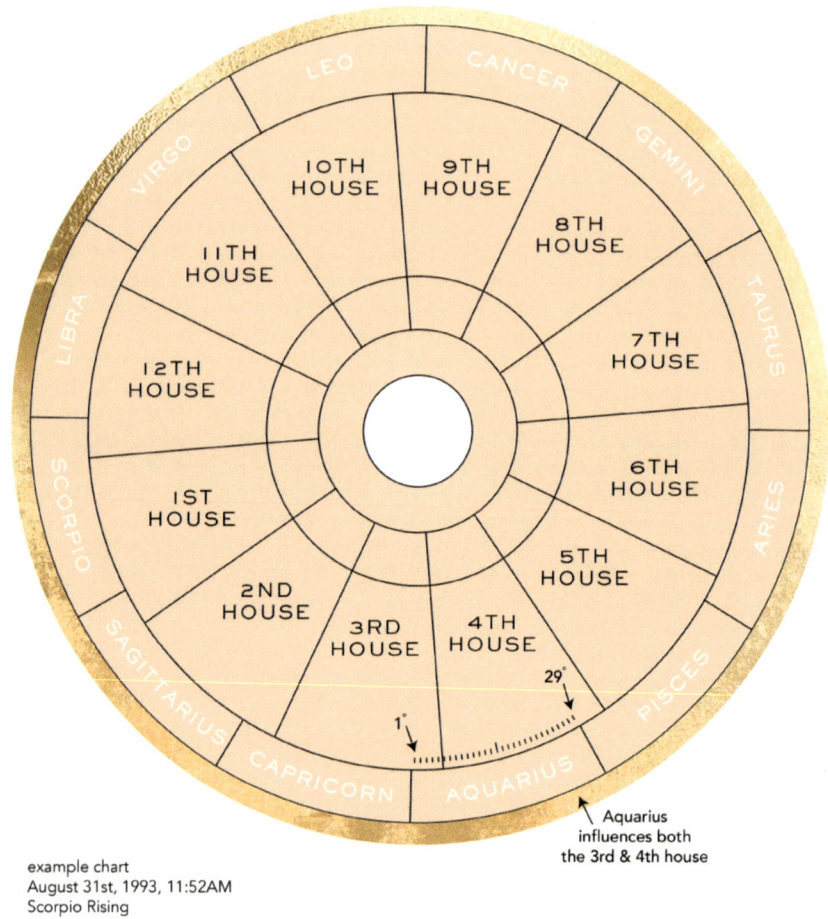

example chart
August 31st, 1993, 11:52AM
Scorpio Rising

Understanding the astrological energies involved is the first step to working with the energy of the Full Moon. If you want to go further in your exploration of the Full Moon's energy, it's important to understand astrological houses. We each have a natal chart that captures a picture of the sky when we were born. Our chart is composed of 360° cut into twelve pieces. It looks like a pie with each 30° piece representing a house. We have twelve houses. Each house rules an area of life. We have a house that rules our relationships, a house that rules communications, a house that rules personal growth, and so on. Houses dictate how we show up in the world. So while the Sun or Moon sign represents an aspect of personality, our houses are where that part of ourselves shows up and acts in the world.

Our houses are governed by the twelve zodiac signs, which are also 30°. The order of the signs in your chart begins with your ascendant, or rising, sign. This is the constellation that was rising on the horizon when you were born. It begins your natal chart and governs your first house. The rest of the houses follow the order of the zodiac. Most of us have an overlap of signs and houses, with two zodiac signs contacting one house. This occurs because a chart generally does not start at the beginning of the sign. If the horizon line hits any degree other than the first one, it shifts the whole chart, meaning two signs cover each house. For instance, if a chart begins at 5° Scorpio, then Scorpio and Sagittarius would contact the first house, Sagittarius and Capricorn would contact the second, Capricorn and Aquarius would contact the third, Aquarius and Pisces would contact the 4th, and so on.

Everyone's chart includes all twelve zodiac signs. You can look up your chart at astro-charts.com or another charting site of your choice. Find your house or houses ruled by Aquarius. We all have a house or part of a house governed by Aquarius. You'll see the signs on the outside of the wheel and the house numbers on the innermost circle. To be more exact, find the house that holds the first degree of Aquarius (that's the side of Aquarius closest to Capricorn) for the first Full Moon in Aquarius, and the house that holds the last degree of Aquarius (closest to Pisces) for the second Full Moon in Aquarius. These are the houses each Full Moon will transit and activate in your life. Learning our houses is how we begin to understand how each Full Moon affects us.

The below horoscopes are based on the house Aquarius governs for you. They can be used for both Full Moons in Aquarius. You most likely will need to read two description to fully understand the effects of each Full Moon on your life.

Aquarius First House: The First House influences your identity and how you project yourself to the outside world. It guides how you define yourself and what definitions you allow other people to see. In many ways, your first house is the mask you wear around people who do not know you intimately. It also informs your choices about who you show up as in the world. With Aquarius here, you appear eccentric in your personality. You are outspoken and enjoy defining yourself as someone who goes against the grain of society. You stand up for your beliefs and expect others to follow. During this Full Moon, focus on what you may be holding back from showing to the world. How can you shatter even more expectations placed upon you and shine your truest colors?

Aquarius Second House: The Second House influences your perception of resources. It governs your self-esteem and self-worth. It also influences how much you rely on material possessions to create a sense of self-respect. On a more mundane level, the second house governs your possessions and the choices you make around finances. The house also informs your concepts of abundance. With Aquarius here, you place value on your ability to think outside the box. You are highly creative, especially when it comes to problem-solving. You may even attempt to tear down conventional ideas about money and how to accumulate it. You are resourceful in the way you acquire money, and you view abundance from many different perspectives. During this Full Moon, break through conditioned patterns of worth and finances. Acknowledge that what you may have been taught isn't what you really believe.

Aquarius Third House: The Third House influences your communication and methods of sharing information, including how you listen. It also governs how you form your perceptions, then express them to the world. With Aquarius in this house, you take a unique approach to conversations. You are not afraid to say what you mean and voice your truth. You may even find yourself leading large groups of people through speech. You have a way with words that helps other people understand concepts in a new light. During this Full Moon break free of any limitations that you or society has placed on your voice. Feel into the power of your expressions. Use your imagination in speaking with others and raise the vibration of the conversation.

HOUSESCOPES

Aquarius Fourth House: The Fourth House influences your home life, including your internal sense of home. It governs your relationships with the most intimate people in your life—your family. It also influences how you take care of yourself, how you listen to your intuition, and what you allow yourself to feel. With Aquarius in this house, you have an unconventional definition of home and family. Allow yourself to live the life you most aligned with, no matter what others may say. If your biological family isn't supportive of who you are, find a soul family that gives you a true sense of belonging. During this Full Moon, release anything that restricts your feelings and makes you feel unaccepted. Open yourself up to the idea that "home" means different things and find places, people, and groups that feel like home to your heart.

Aquarius Fifth House: The Fifth House influences your creativity, ability to play, and capacity for joy. It also is where you'll find your inner child and the path to healing that person so you can experience complete happiness. This house reminds you to smile, celebrate life, and trust the world again after you've been hurt. With Aquarius here, you crave unique adventures and people to enjoy them with. Your friends are an important piece of your life, and you're often the leader of the pack. You restore your spirit with others and remember who you are in the presence of people who love you. Celebrate this Full Moon with other people. Connect fully with your joy and the people who remind you to enjoy life. Let this enjoyment heal you and expand your love of the world.

Aquarius Sixth House: The Sixth House influences how you serve others through your unique skills. It governs how you help others and yourself heal. It also guides how you approach organizations, including time, schedules, and routines. With Aquarius here, you have an interesting approach to life. You avoid mundane routines and thrive in what appears to others as chaotic systems. When left unrestricted, you find ways to serve humanity by envisioning a future that others fail to see. You bring your visionary gifts to the world in the form of healing and energy work, which helps others step into the future. During the Full Moon, break through any self-imposed limitations and free yourself to share your visions with others. Release the fear of rejection and know that you can heal people where others have failed.

Aquarius Seventh House: The Seventh House influences your relationships and partnerships. It affects how you define yourself in a relationship and how you hold onto your identity when merging energy with another. With Aquarius here, you may find it challenging to compromise with another. You have a strong sense of self and fear losing it in a partnership. You insert your unique personality in every situation. Sometimes you are met with acceptance, other times with resentment. You also view partnerships in terms of energetic alignment. You need to be with partners who understand how to tune into your frequency and not try to lower it. Ideally, you want someone who raises your vibration as you do for them. During this Full Moon, break through anything that holds you back from showing up as your full self in a relationship. Understand that you may require unions that defy convention, and that's ok. That's you.

Aquarius Eighth House: The Eighth House influences your personal growth and how you transform as an individual. It guides you in processing information that helps you evolve and shift into the next cycle of being. It also governs how you navigate challenging times in your life and use them as fuel for your evolution. With Aquarius in this house, you attract situations that force you out of your habitual thinking and conditioned patterns. You are constantly seeking new adventures that will help you thrive. You may be brought challenging situations that ask you to use your imagination, find your power, and speak your truth. Your growth defies convention but you have the potential to energetically evolve greatly in this lifetime. During this Full Moon, release any hesitation you may feel when faced with a new opportunity for growth. Embrace every challenge knowing that it is through pressure that you evolve the most.

Aquarius Ninth House: The Ninth House influences your travel, quest for knowledge, and search for ultimate truths. It governs your ability to leap into the unknown and guides you in integrating new experiences. It is also the house of travel and long trips. This house motivates you to break away from your everyday routine and experience the world. With Aquarius in this house, you seek the unexpected. You have an adventurous spirit and thrive when given the freedom to traverse the world. You take unexpected leaps of faith, which others generally won't understand. Stay true to yourself and always stand up for what you believe. On the Full Moon, release anything holding you back from finding your true freedom. Embrace a leap into the unknown even if it rattles your sense of self. You'll always find your way home.

Aquarius Tenth House: The Tenth House influences your career and reputation. It governs how you portray your inner world to the outer world and what you choose to show others. This house governs your integrity and what you do to stay aligned with your values. It also guides how well you handle rules, regulations, and authority. With Aquarius here, you do not conform easily to societal pressure. You are your own leader and may even resent positions of power, always striving to redefine the rules that govern all of us. Your career may take the form of an activist or a person who strives to mend broken societal systems. You also do best when you work for yourself, having no one to answer to. On the Full Moon, embrace your life's work. Feel into what your soul wants to do on this planet and the mission you are on in this lifetime. Know that your career path may be unconventional, and that's ok.

Aquarius Eleventh House: The Eleventh House influences your sense of belonging. It is Aquarius's home. The Eleventh House and Aquarius share common traits, and it is here we can see the qualities of Aquarius stand up and act. Traditionally known as the house of friends, the eleventh governs your outer circle of friends, including acquaintances. The people in this circle are not necessarily intimate friends, but rather people you share interests with and who support your visions. With Aquarius ruling this house in your chart, you seek out communities who understand your visions. You are often the leader of any group and speak your truth with ease. You must be cautious to avoid trying to fit in with people who don't align with you; instead, seek out those who genuinely appreciate your uniqueness. During the Full Moon, release any need to please people who don't understand you. Be you and know that the people who get the real you will show up in one form or another.

Aquarius Twelfth House: The Twelfth House influences how you integrate spirituality into your life. It also governs how you channel your spiritual growth into helping others heal. This house asks you to take a wide-eyed view of your life and place your actions within the larger framework of the Universe. With Aquarius in this house, you take an open-minded approach to all types of spirituality. You may even look for the most progressive one, searching the world far and wide for spiritual paths. You have the ability to then use what you've learned to help people evolve through healing. You present unconventional solutions that use imagination and thought forms that defy most people's understand of the Universe. Even if others don't fully understand your visions, they still are powerful for healing the collective. During the Full Moon, embrace your creativity and capacity to heal. Share it with others and allow yourself to be seen for the powerful being you are.

You can look up what house Aquarius rules in your chart, at astro-charts.com

AQUARIUS LUNAR FLOW

Aquarius rules the ankles, shins, calves, and circulatory system. This energy reminds you to stand tall in your truth and always keep your energy flowing so new inspiration can enter your field. The Full Moon brings you an abundance of energy to work with in your body. The following sequence is designed to help circulate and integrate the many vibrations of the Aquarius Full Moon. You can practice this sequence on both Full Moons in Aquarius to strengthen your spirit and open your heart.

Dandasana Ankle Sequence

Begin in a seated position with your legs straight in front of you. Lengthen through your spine and reach through the crown of your head, keeping your back straight. Sit on a pillow to elevate your hips if you feel yourself hunching over in your spine. Have your arms by your sides, palms pressing into the floor, shoulders relaxed. While keeping your legs straight, flex and point through your feet. Inhale deeply as you flex, spreading your toes, and exhale as you point, pairing your breath with the movement. Take about 10 full breaths. Then begin to make ankle rolls with your foot to one side. Rotate your foot about 10 times, then switch sides. Next, attempt to touch the soles of your feet together while keeping your legs straight. Then reverse the movement, attempting to press the tops of your feet together. They won't touch, but your ankle will gain a new stretch. Do about 10 rounds of these.

Cat/Cow with Spinal Rolls

Come to your hands and knees. On inhale, arch through your spine, lifting your head. On exhale, round through your spine and look at your navel. Continue this for 5 breaths, then begin to make barrel rolls with your rib cage, circling first to the left and then to the right. Continue for 1 minute, then come into a Downward-Facing Dog. Peddle out your feet here, pressing through one foot down to the floor, than through the other. Spend a few breaths here, slightly bending and straightening your knees, and stretching your calves.

Sun Salutation A - 5 Rounds

Stand at the top of your mat, rooting down through your feet to rise through your crown. Inhale and stretch your arms overhead, reaching fingertips to the ceiling. Exhale and fold forward. Inhale and lengthen your back. Exhale and step back to Plank Pose, pressing back through your heels. Lower to the ground, inhale, and reach your chest up for Cobra Pose, legs on the ground. Exhale into Downward Dog Pose. Stay here for 5 breaths and feel your entire body expand. On exhale, step to the top of your mat. Inhale and lengthen through your spine. Exhale and fold forward. Inhale and come up to standing, reaching your arms overhead. Exhale with your hands to your heart. Pause for a moment and feel yourself centered throughout your body. Complete 4 more rounds.

AQUARIUS LUNAR FLOW

Sun Salutation B - 3 Rounds

Stand at the top of your mat. Inhale, stretch your arms overhead, and bend your knees into Chair Pose. Exhale and fold forward. Inhale and lengthen your back. Exhale, step into Plank Pose, and lower halfway to Chatarunga (like a push-up with elbows into your ribs). Inhale and reach your chest up for Upward-Facing Dog with everything off the ground except your hands and feet. Exhale and go to Downward Dog Pose. Inhale, stepping your left foot forward to Warrior 1. With your back foot flat at a 45° angle, bend into your front knee and lift your arms to the sky. Take 5 breaths here. Exhale, release into Plank, and then lower to Chaturanga. Inhale and move to Upward-Facing Dog. Exhale into Downward-Facing Dog. Repeat on your right side, then remain in Downward Dog for 5 breaths. Exhale and step to the top of your mat. Inhale and lengthen through your spine. Exhale and fold forward. Inhale into Chair Pose. Exhale, hands to heart, and breathe at the top of your mat as you feel your energy circulating throughout your body. Complete 2 more rounds.

Tree Pose

Step your feet to the top of the mat, bringing them together. Slowly bring your right foot up for Tree Pose, placing it on the inside of your left leg. Press firmly down through your standing leg, imagining roots going down into the Earth and providing you with balance. Reach and lengthen your spine upward, growing taller through your torso as you lift your arms to the sky. Take 5 deep breaths here before switching sides.

Warrior 2 > Extended Warrior > Triangle > Wide-Angle Forward Bend

Step your right foot back for Warrior 2 with your left leg forward. Have your back foot almost parallel with the edge of your mat, turning it in slightly. Reach your arms out to either side as you inhale, bending deeply in your front leg. Take 5 full breaths here, reaching through your fingers and lengthening through your spine. On inhale, straighten your front leg, then re-bend it on exhale. Place your left elbow on your front thigh, pressing into it while dragging your shoulder down your back. Reach your right arm overhead, in line with your ear, and rotate your torso to the right for Extended Warrior. Feel your right side lengthen as you stretch from heel to fingertip. After 5 breaths, lift your torso. On exhale, straighten through your front leg, reach forward, fold over your front leg, and rotate your torso to the right for Triangle Pose. Reach your right arm up to the sky and focus on your middle fingertip. Stay here for 5 breaths. Feel your feet and legs grounding you as you open up through your heart and spine. On exhale, bring your torso back upright. Turn your feet parallel for a Wide-Angle Fold. Reach your arms back and clasp your hands. Inhale and lift your chest, exhale, and fold forward. Breathe here as your spine and shoulders release. After 5 breaths, inhale and lift your torso back upright. Release your hands and rotate your feet to practice on the other side.

Chair Pose > Forward Bend

Return to the front of your mat. Keep your feet together and bend deeply into your knees as if you were sitting in a chair. Reach your arms upward to the sky and look up. Feel your belly drawing in, helping to direct your tailbone to the floor. Take 5 breaths and feel the strength of your legs. Inhale, come back up to standing, exhale, and fold forward for 5 breaths, allowing your torso to lengthen again. On inhale, slowly roll up to standing.

Savasana

Stretch both your legs out long on your mat and place your palms facing upward in a receptive motion. Feel your entire body supported by the ground beneath you. Let your breath become natural and feel the energy circulating through you from your practice. Allow your mind to be still and your body to be calm.

I ACCEPT MYSELF AS I AM TODAY

FULL MOON MEDITATION

Yogic Three-Part Breathwork

Aquarius is ruled by Air and reminds us of the importance of our breath. On both Full Moons in Aquarius, it's important to spend time with your breath, using it to help circulate energy throughout your body. Air also connects each of us, and when we focus on it, we strengthen our bonds with the collective energy. The following breathwork helps soothe the mind, calm the nervous system, and move energy throughout the entire body.

Start in a relaxed position, either seated upright or lying down. Place your right hand on your heart and your left hand on your belly. Think of your torso as three parts. Deeply inhale into your chest, feeling it expand side to side, then fill the space of your upper abdomen. Send the breath into your belly, extending it out like a balloon. Slowly release the breath first from your belly, then your upper abdomen, and finally your chest, feeling a complete exhalation. This is one complete breath. Continue breathing like this for 5 minutes.

Self-Acceptance Affirmation Meditation

The following meditation is a set of affirmations for you to repeat. Each affirmation guides you in releasing judgment of yourself to allow your authentic self to emerge.

Allow your breath to become natural, feeling a smooth, even inhalation and exhalation. Allow your entire body to relax. In working with this meditation, first read the affirmation, then close your eyes and say it to yourself as you take a breath in and out.

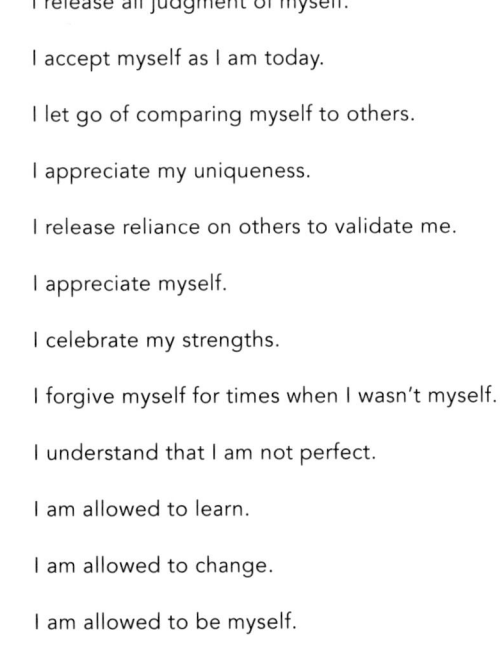

I release all judgment of myself.

I accept myself as I am today.

I let go of comparing myself to others.

I appreciate my uniqueness.

I release reliance on others to validate me.

I appreciate myself.

I celebrate my strengths.

I forgive myself for times when I wasn't myself.

I understand that I am not perfect.

I am allowed to learn.

I am allowed to change.

I am allowed to be myself.

I love myself unconditionally.

CIRCLE SET UP

You can use this circle set up for both Full Moons in Aquarius. On each of these Full Moons, we are working with the elements of Air from Aquarius and Fire from Leo. Feel into these elements when creating your space. When Fire meets Air, sparks fly. Choose a space that feels grounded and connected to Mother Earth to help contain the Fire element, but also allow the Air element to breathe new life into your ritual space. You can practice alone or in community; it's entirely up to you. Due to the nature of these Full Moons, you may want to spend the first one with others, while honoring the second one alone. Aquarius is a very social sign and the energy supports gathering with others. If you practice with other people, be sure to choose people you feel at home with—people who give you a true sense of belonging in their presence.

CIRCLE SET UP

Along with the Earth element, incorporate the rest of the elements into your space. If possible, build a fire outside, which you can use for a releasing ritual. You can also light candles to represent Fire. For Air, incorporate auric sprays, feathers to fan the smudge sticks, and even wind chimes to hear the air moving around you. Use crystals to help bring in more of the Earth element, and call in energies that align with their vibration. When placing crystals, allow the crystal to choose its location, using your intuition as a guide. Place crystals in the middle of the circle in the form of a crystal grid and around the perimeter of the space.

Crystals that align with the energy of Aquarius are Peacock Ore, Aquamarine, Goldstone, and Kambabla Jasper. They will help you feel into your unique talent and contribution to the collective. Crystals for Leo are Morganite, Tiger's Eye, Citrine, and Carnelian. They will help you love yourself unconditionally and express your true creativity. You can also incorporate flowers for both Aquarius and Leo, including gladiolas, bird of paradise, and carnations. Bring in the element of Water through a room diffuser, a vase, or a metal bowl containing water. Gather all of your supplies and start to build your circle.

Create an outline with your objects, anchoring the four directions—North, South, East, and West—with either a crystal or candle. If you are creating an altar, set it up in the westerly part of the circle, as this direction helps energies release. On your altar you can place pictures of images that inspire or guide you. Also place items that represent your past or things you want to leave behind. Additionally, place candles and crystals here that facilitate release, such as Obsidian or Shungite. Once the perimeter is set, cleanse the area with a dried herb. For the eclectic energy of Aquarius, try using sweetgrass or rosemary, or both. Begin cleansing at the easterly point, moving to the South, West, and North, then back to the East. Imagine a white light encasing the circle, protecting it from any external energies. Before your guests enter, cleanse them too from head to toe. Don't forget to cleanse yourself. Once you have all entered the circle, pause for a moment to let the energy settle before you begin.

Follow your intuitive guidance when leading a circle. Begin by having each member introduce themself. Talk about the astrological energy of the day and how it is affecting each one of you. Share and learn from each other about your unique experiences with this Full Moon. Give plenty of space for each person to speak. Follow your conversation with the meditation practice in this book to calm the mind. You can then explore the rest of the practices. Do them alone, and share as much or as little as you wish with the group. Go over the questions and continue to learn from each other's perspectives. Finally, pull some cards to tune into your intuitive guidance.

After you've completed the practices, take three pieces of paper. On one, write something you are releasing from your past this Full Moon. On the second, write an intention you are calling in that will help you move forward on your path. On the third, write what you are grateful for tonight. Gather all the releasing notes and either burn them (safely) or rip them to shreds. Gather the intention notes and place them under a crystal in the most easterly corner of your home. Leave them there for a week. Pass the gratitude notes to the person on the left, then have everyone take their neighbor's home. Sharing in others' gratitude is a beautiful way to merge our energy into the collective. End the circle by giving thanks to everyone who attended and to yourself for showing up.

CARD READING

Reading Cards is a beautiful way to access your intuition and tap into your, and the Universe's, higher wisdom. Anyone can pull cards, as long as you are willing to receive the information they provide. You need no prior experience, or training, just an open and clear mind.

You may use any cards you like for this practice, including but not limited to: Tarot Cards, Animal Medicine Cards, Oracle Cards or any Affirmation Cards. You also can pull cards from a few decks to gain different perspectives. If you are new to card pulling, try to ask only one deck the same question, as asking different decks the same question can become quite confusing. Below are some general guidelines on how to pull cards. Please improvise as needed and above anything else, listen to your intuition.

Clear Your Mind
A settled, grounded mind is essential for pulling cards. The last thing you want is random thoughts running around when you are trying to receive clear answers from yourself. Practice the breath work and meditation in this workbook to prepare and settle your mind. You may also clear your mind using sound frequencies through singing bowls. These can either be crystal or metal bowls. Play the bowl, or bowls, for about 3-5 minutes to help rid your mind of external noise as you focus on the harmony of the sound.

CARD READING

Pick Your Deck
There are many different decks out there. You can choose as many as you like. Know, though, that they each provide you a different energy or medicine. Tarot Cards are the most popular and should be used carefully. Although very useful, Tarot cards can give the wrong impression if you interpret them harshly. Animal Medicine cards offer different types of messages from the animal realm which can help align with the spirit of nature. These cards give you the medicine you need to apply to your situation or question. Affirmation cards provide you with guidance in the form of words or phrases. When reading these cards, it is best to meditate on what the affirmation means for you. It is also helpful to repeat the affirmation a few times and see how it makes you feel. There are many other cards you can experiment with, like Goddess Cards, Angel Cards, and so on. The important thing to remember with any card is that they each have different angles and sides. There are often a few interpretations of the same card.

Shuffle
Shuffle the cards the easiest way for you. Some cards are smaller and can be shuffled like a regular deck of playing cards, while others with take some effort. If all else fails, spread them out on the floor in front of you then regather them. Keep a clear mind while shuffling. You can also repeat " I am open to receiving guidance and intuition." Refrain from asking your questions until the next step.

Aquarius Card Questions
You are free to ask the deck any questions you need answers to on this Full Moon. The following questions are meant to help you harness the energy of Aquarius through the cards to clarify some of these energies in your mind. This is a three-part card reading, where you'll ask the deck three questions. Before beginning, spread your freshly shuffled cards in a wide arc in front of you. Use your left middle finger to choose the card, first waving your hand slowly over the cards. You'll feel a magnetic pull, or slight tingle, in your fingertip when you hover over the right card. Chose one card at a time, taking a moment to breathe in between questions. Keep the cards flipped over until you pull all three.

What energy will help me break free of conditioned patterns?

What energy will help me find and speak my truth?

What energy will help me align with my authentic self?

Take Them In
Once you have your cards, flip them over. Before looking up their meaning, sit with them for a moment and allow them to speak to you. Intuit your own meaning and interpretation of the card. What is the card trying to tell you? What are you trying to tell yourself? After a few moments with the cards, look up their meaning. Sit with that information, merging it with your intuitive meaning of the cards.

As with everything, enjoy this process. Do not worry if you are doing it right or wrong. Just follow your intuition, and trust the journey. Accept the cards you are dealt and use their energy wisely to help guide you when you need it the most.

20

THERE IS NO GREATER POWER THAN KNOWING WHO YOU ARE.

SPIRIT DAUGHTER

AQUARIUS PRACTICES

Throughout this Full Moon, we are working with the energies of Aquarius and Leo. Both of these signs want us to understand our most authentic selves, accept ourselves, and love ourselves unconditionally. Aquarius takes this further by asking us to show our true selves to the world and speak our truths, even if others don't understand it. This Full Moon is an opportunity to shed any behaviors or patterns that block you from being yourself. It is also a chance to understand your emotional attachments to certain ways of thinking or societal programing.

Much like a computer, we are a series of programming that has been placed upon us. Unlike a computer, though, we have the choice to break free of our programming and live in the moment. To understand your programming, notice the reactions you have to situations, emotions, and other people. When you are operating from your programs, your responses are automatic. They arise from a subconscious place and barely give you a chance to acknowledge them before affecting your energy.

A conditioned response is learned. We pick them up from our parents, teachers, and society. Some programming serves us well, while others become quickly outdated. Society evolves by breaking its previous programming. What was true twenty years ago is no longer true today and deserves a new, updated response. In order to honor the person you are today and the state of the world today, you need to update your programming to reflect the current moment.

The Aquarius Full Moon is an opportunity to observe your patterns, understand their origin, and break them. Then you can form new responses based on your authentic truth, not someone else's before you. It's a time to feel your truth and your heart, then act from that place. This process takes much conscious effort and will most likely not be accomplished in a day. Begin, though, on this Full Moon to bring your awareness to those automatic responses that control you without you even knowing it. Decide if they really resonate with who you are or if you need to release them to make space for actions that reflect a newer version of yourself.

Once you've started breaking through the programming, patterns, and reactions that are not really yours, you will evolve into the person you are meant to be. The challenge then becomes, showing this new version of yourself to the world— including the people who taught you the old programming. As we change and evolve, some people in our lives may not accept our changes. When loved ones and people close to us change, even for the better, it can be off-putting and frightening. As you align with your authentic self and shed outdated behaviors, you may be confronted with confused expressions and questioning glances. Furthermore, some people may not be comfortable with or accept you when you speak your truth. Know that all of these behaviors are ok. You do not need to defend yourself for growing or aligning with your heart. Resist the urge to conform to others' expectations and stay true to yourself. Align with the vibrations of Leo to hold your head high and have the courage to be yourself. Align with Aquarius to realize you are transforming the collective by living in your truth. Align with both to be a leader and lead the collective to a new consciousness by showing up as yourself.

In addition to feeling your truth this Full Moon, practice seeing yourself in another. Aquarius reminds us that we are all connected. We are all made of the same energy. Our hearts are all part of the same interconnected field of energy. Look around at people you know and people you don't. Acknowledge that you and another person are the same. You may differ in talents, looks, and lifestyle, but deep down we are all humans living on this planet with beating hearts and vast energy fields. Feel the oneness with everyone and allow it to open your heart to the highest vibration of all: unconditional love.

AQUARIUS PRACTICES

You can perform the following practices on or around the Full Moon. Take your time with them and allow the answers to surface without forcing them.

1. What are some patterns or behaviors in your life that you embrace but that don't align with who you are? Where do these patterns come from? Where did you learn them?

_____

_____

_____

_____

_____

_____

_____

_____

_____

_____

_____

_____

_____

_____

_____

_____

_____

_____

_____

_____

_____

AQUARIUS PRACTICES

2. What emotions surface when you think about breaking free of patterns taught to you? How do you feel about evolving past the conditioned responses you learned from the world around you?

_____

_____

_____

_____

_____

_____

_____

_____

_____

_____

_____

_____

_____

_____

_____

_____

_____

_____

_____

_____

_____

_____

_____

_____

_____

AQUARIUS PRACTICES

3. What are some reactions you have to current conditions that belong in the past? How can you become more present and give space to your reactions?

_____

_____

_____

_____

_____

_____

_____

_____

_____

_____

_____

_____

_____

_____

_____

_____

_____

_____

_____

_____

_____

_____

_____

_____

AQUARIUS PRACTICES

4. What empowers you to be yourself? What disempowers you?
   How can you shift away from things that disempower you?

_____

_____

_____

_____

_____

_____

_____

_____

_____

_____

_____

_____

_____

_____

_____

_____

_____

_____

_____

_____

_____

_____

_____

_____

_____

AQUARIUS PRACTICES

5. What helps you feel your truth? What or who reminds you of who
you are at your core, including your values, your heart, and your
unique ideas?

_____

_____

_____

_____

_____

_____

_____

_____

_____

_____

_____

_____

_____

_____

_____

_____

_____

_____

_____

_____

_____

_____

_____

_____

AQUARIUS PRACTICES

6. What are some things that unique about yourself that no one else possesses?

_____

_____

_____

_____

_____

_____

_____

_____

_____

_____

_____

_____

_____

_____

_____

_____

_____

_____

_____

_____

_____

_____

_____

_____

_____

AQUARIUS PRACTICES

7. How does your presence enhance the collective? What do you, or
   could you, contribute that no one else can?

_____

_____

_____

_____

_____

_____

_____

_____

_____

_____

_____

_____

_____

_____

_____

_____

_____

_____

_____

_____

_____

_____

_____

_____

_____

AQUARIUS PRACTICES

8. How do you react with others who don't accept you? Do you people-please? Or become aloof?

_____

_____

_____

_____

_____

_____

_____

_____

_____

_____

_____

_____

_____

_____

_____

_____

_____

_____

_____

_____

_____

_____

_____

_____

_____

AQUARIUS PRACTICES

9. How can you honor and love who you are while extending compassion to the other person?

_____

_____

_____

_____

_____

_____

_____

_____

_____

_____

_____

10. How can you stand in your truth with an open heart?

_____

_____

_____

_____

_____

_____

_____

_____

_____

_____

_____

AQUARIUS PRACTICES

11. List three people who seem very different from you. How can you see yourself in them? What are the commonalities? What are you assuming and what is true about the other person?

_____

_____

_____

_____

_____

_____

_____

_____

_____

_____

_____

12. How can you lead every choice for yourself and the collective from a place of love? What would that look like in your world?

_____

_____

_____

_____

_____

_____

_____

_____

_____

_____

LAST QUARTER
IN TAURUS

JULY 31

The dance of the lunar cycle continues as the Moon makes her way another quarter around the Earth, bringing us our second Half Moon of the lunar cycle. Last quarters provide us with final moments of release before we begin again with the New Moon.

Taurus is the sign of the peaceful bull, content with spending the day in nature observing its beauty. Taurus reminds us to enjoy the simple pleasures of life, soaking them in with all five senses. It also teaches us that in being fully present with these sensations, we have access to our most creative selves. It is from stillness we bring forth beauty.

While enjoying the comforts of life is a good thing, we must be careful not to become attached to them. When we do, these simple pleasures become limiting comfort zones that prevent our growth. This can include habitual ways of thinking and behaving, which may feel good because they are familiar. But they are not the path of the soul's evolution.

This last quarter is coming at the height of Leo Season, allowing us to shed what is familiar to grow and evolve. It asks us what attachments are blocking our full self-expression and how we can step away from them. Taurus likes security, but Leo is asking us to do things that inspire courage. This last quarter shows us where our courage and our comfort collide and how we respond to their confrontation. Ask yourself today what limiting habits (including relationships) you are holding onto out of comfort and fear of the unfamiliar. Can you let them go to step courageously into a new vibration?

What are you willing to let go this
Last Quarter Moon to allow yourself to
receive new energy?

AFFIRMATIONS

Write down energies that raise your vibration and align you with your most authentic self. These can be love, gratitude, contentment—anything that makes you feel lighter, clearer, and grounded in your body.

_____

_____

_____

_____

_____

_____

_____

_____

_____

_____

Now write three to five affirmations using the energies listed above. Create "I am statements," which you can tell yourself to help bring you back to center and raise your vibration when needed.

_____

_____

_____

_____

_____

_____

_____

_____

_____

_____

_____

HAPPY
FULL MOON!

Thank you to everyone who supported and purchased this workbook.

Special Thanks to Rebecca Reitz (rebeccareitz.com, @becca_reitz) for her beautiful artwork on the cover, page 2, 4, 6, 14, 20, 32.

For a monthly subscription contact hello@spiritdaughter.com or visit www.spiritdaughter.com.

Disclaimer: The exercises and yoga sequences in this book are physical activities that should be performed carefully to avoid injury. You agree to accept all risks and release Spirit Daughter and any guest instructors from any and all liabilities. Please take care and enjoy.

Follow along our journey on IG:
@spiritdaughter

We always love seeing your photos & hearing about your experiences with the workbooks! Tag us to be featured on our community page:
@spiritdaughtercollective